JANE AUSTEN'S

A converted posting inn, at the j̶... was the happy, secure home of Jane Austen during eight productive years, the years in which she wrote or revised all six of her completed novels.

Today, Chawton is visited by Jane's admirers from all over the world. However, the museum in the former Austen house is not the only attraction of this compact little village, so easily explored on foot. Physically, the village has barely been altered since the days of the Regency. With the help of her letters, and certain other sources, the world of Jane Austen can still be vividly conjured up. It is also possible to glimpse here an even older pattern of English rural society. From Chawton's splendid 'Great House', life in the village was governed, until relatively recently, by the lord of the manor, who also exercised a controlling influence on the nearby parish church. For example, until the outbreak of the Second World War, the 'squire' ensured that a Curfew Bell was rung here every evening at 8 p.m. (33 tolls, plus the day and the month), for the benefit of those, presumably few, of his tenants without the advantage of a watch or calendar.

In the small cluster of houses that constitutes the village centre, the handsome villas of the gentry are juxtaposed with the cramped cottages which were once the preserve of the poor. Some of these cottages are thatched, and picturesquely bent with age. There are a pub, a school and a cricket pitch to complete the picture, and little by way of modern development to detract from it.

In surveying nearly a thousand years of Chawton's recorded history, this book attempts to re-create the landscape that Jane Austen would have known. It is intended not only for Jane's admirers, but for all who live in or visit Chawton, and who have an interest in its past.

A map of the village is to be found on pages 22 and 23.

TO JO, WITH MUCH LOVE

First published 1998
Second edition 2003

Designed by Martin Atcherley and
published by the author at The Old Rectory,
Sherborne St John, Hants. RG24 9JD

Printed by Creeds the Printers,
Broadoak, Bridport, Dorset. DT6 5NL

ISBN 0 9534428 4 5
(ISBN 0 9534428 0 2 paperback, 1st edition)

ACKNOWLEDGEMENTS

The author gratefully acknowledges the following for the information, hospitality, support and constructive criticism that they have variously provided: Miss Jean K. Bowden, Mr Tom Carpenter, Miss Julian Chrysostomides, Dr Michael Clanchy, Mrs Dee Cook, Archivist of the Society of Apothecaries, Mrs Caroline Dibden, Mr and Mrs Peter Gannon, Mrs Violet Hunt, Mr and Mrs Nicholas Kerridge, Mr Richard Knight, Mr Adam Knight, Father Michael McGreevy, Mr Arthur Page, Mr Mark Pearson, Mr Michael Sanders, and Colonel and Mrs David Whitaker.

I. 'THE CORNER HOUSE BY THE POND'

MRS GEORGE AUSTEN and her daughters, Cassandra and Jane, came to live at Chawton on 7 July 1809. Like the Dashwoods in *Sense and Sensibility*, they were poor relations 'in need of a dwelling', who had depended on the beneficence of a kindly relative (in the person of Jane's own brother Edward) for accommodation. With its eight bedrooms, and additional servant's quarters, their new home would have been considered spacious enough by most people, even if, to ladies of Jane's class, it was 'but a cottage'.

The building had originated, around the year 1700, as a farmhouse. Its conversion into the private residence of gentlefolk had taken place relatively recently. For the Austen ladies, there was no forgetting that, in between, 'the Cottage' had served briefly as an alehouse, an indignity that lingered in official descriptions of the place as the 'Late Inn'.

Although the village of Chawton is by-passed by the traffic of today, the parish has at all times in its history been traversed by one or more major arteries of communication. On its corner site, the building had been ideally situated for a posting inn. What sort of traffic would it have catered for in its early history?

The London to Gosport road, on to which the building opened, was an ancient 'King's highway', but the **Winchester Road** (properly called the

'Shrave'), which forks off to the west at this point, must originally have been a mere lane. This, surely, was the road to Ropley, and intended for mainly local use. Its transformation into a major thoroughfare dates from 1753, when Parliament recognised the need for a widened and properly maintained route from Bagshot in Surrey, through Farnham and Alton, and on, through New Alresford, to Winchester.

The old Alton to Winchester road, which the Act of 1753 describes as 'deep and ruinous, and dangerous to Carriages and Travellers', had avoided the village altogether. It had passed instead through the high ground in the north-west of the parish, skirting the entire southern boundary of **Chawton Park Wood**, along a ridgeway that had doubtless been carved out in Saxon times. Beyond Chawton Park, it took the route of still existing lanes through Medstead, Old Alresford, Itchen Stoke and the Worthys, finally approaching Winchester from the north. At the Chawton end, the course of this once broad highway is marked, somewhat approximately, by a **public footpath**. However, the traces of up to eight parallel trackways can still be seen in the undergrowth, a little to the south of **Chawton Park Farm**. The old road emerged from the eastern end of the Wood to become what is now **Chawton Park Road**, **Butts Road** and, eventually, **Alton High Street**.

The historical interest of the now deserted track through the Wood is probably little appreciated today. In the early part of the 19th century, however, the redundant ridgeway must still have been discernably a road. Cobbett, a contemporary of Jane Austen, was to describe the passage of the old highway through 'this lofty land which is, perhaps, the finest *beech-wood* in all England'. The road is often described as being part of the old 'Pilgrim's Way'. This was the route by which the medieval devotees of St Thomas Becket (many of them having crossed from France) are said to have journeyed to Canterbury from Southampton or Winchester, in a manner made familiar by Chaucer through his *Canterbury Tales*. There is little evidence, however, to support the tradition of an established pilgrim road.

An association with pilgrims might more credibly be inferred for the present 'Winchester Road' through Chawton, from the fact that it was once – and at the Four Marks end still is – called the 'Shrave'. Another theory is that the ridgeway route was a summerway. In the 13th and 14th centuries, however, travellers would have had good reason to prefer the low road, or 'Shrave', through the village, for the 'Pass of Alton' – the point where the main road descended from the wooded heights onto Chawton Park Road – was a notorious nest of robbers. Among them may have been Sir Adam de Gurdon, a prototype of Robin Hood, who was famously rooted out of his lair by the future King Edward I in 1265. A baggage-train of Henry III had been attacked here in 1261, prompting a scheme to widen this section of the road. Despite such measures, the merchants on their way to and from Winchester would continue to be a target for ambush, even if, as Langland observes in *Piers Plowman*,

'Ye, thorugh the pass of Aultone
Poverte myght passe, withoute perile of robbynge'.

Transport on these roads consisted solely of horses and wagons, but most would have travelled on foot. The stage coach, a late 17th-century innovation, must have heightened the need for improved highways. The 'Alton Machine', a stage coach which, in 1750, could make the journey to London in a day, was a pioneering form of public transport. The Act of 1753, of course, introduced additional traffic to Chawton by diverting the main Winchester Road to this junction. In or soon after 1769, when Jane Austen's future home was turned into the 'New Inn', the demand for shelter and cheer from travellers through Chawton must therefore have been considerable.

The newly-improved highways were to be 'turnpiked' by the business consortia who had taken responsibility for them. Coaches were charged at the rate of a shilling per horse, whereas the toll for any 'horse, mule or ass not drawing' was a penny. Users would be charged only once a day as they travelled, and would therefore be issued with a ticket at their first gate. Although there is no memory here of any toll-gate, 'Chawton Pond' – the 'very considerable pond' beside her house of which Jane Austen wrote in one of her letters – was one of the collecting points. Old photographs and maps show this pond (all-but dry by the second half of the 19th century, and filled in during the 1930s) to have been on the **south side of the fork in the road**, near the corner opposite Jane Austen's house that is now grassed over and paved.

In the event, the 'New Inn' was to be closed after no more than about eighteen years. The parish of Chawton had had a long aversion to pubs, which seem to have been regarded as more trouble than they were worth. Yet the traffic through Chawton, far from being any less, was at its busiest in Jane Austen's day. Indeed, it was detrimental to the family's peace and privacy. They had barely moved into the house when a gentleman passing by in a coach was able to observe them through the **window of the dining-parlour**, 'looking comfortable at breakfast'. Jane's niece, Caroline Austen, refers to 'the close vicinity of the road' as an 'evil' which the ladies were obliged to tolerate. 'The front door opened on the road, a very narrow enclosure of each side protected the house from the possible shock of any runaway vehicle.' She adds, nevertheless, that 'Collyer's daily coach with six horses was a sight to see! and most delightful was it to a child to have the awful stillness of night so frequently broken by the noise of passing carriages, which seemed sometimes, even to shake the bed ...'

A few years after the death of Jane Austen in 1817, the whole of the London to Gosport road was to be 'macadamised', the inventor of the process coming down to supervise the works in person. It is along the newly improved road through Chawton that Joseph Sedley passes, in a post-chaise, in *Vanity Fair*, on a journey which he frequently interrupts for refreshment. By about 1833, however, the scene had been transformed, the coming of the railways (three lines of which branched through the parish of Chawton), having, as Caroline Austen puts it, 'tranquilised' the village.

Chawton's quietude was broken again with the advent of the motor car. It aroused great curiosity when it appeared at Alton in 1897, but in the ensuing decades it was to invade the now-nationalised highways that converged on Chawton, constituting a serious blight on the village. The need for a by-pass was first proposed by the Parish Council in 1932. In 1966, it was reported that motor accidents had become a regular occurrence in the village, whilst the queues of traffic which were held up outside Jane Austen's house on Sunday evenings would regularly extend for hundreds of yards, a situation that would have been considerably worse today.

The much-needed A31 **by-pass**, opened in 1971, skirts the north-western side of the village, cutting it off from Chawton Park Wood. It has been a rather brutal solution, which seems to have placed the requirements of the motorist firmly above those of the pedestrian. The historic A32 London to Gosport road has been mutilated at both ends of the village. On the weekend that followed the opening of the by-pass, only two couples visited a village tea-shop that would normally have expected sixty. The noise from the by-pass is incessant. To follow Jane Austen's footsteps, whether along her regular route, by way of the old main road, into Alton, or by **Mounter's Lane**, at the northern end of the village, up to Chawton Park Wood, it is first necessary to descend into an unexpected **underground passage** – a feature more familiar to the inner city than the countryside – in order to reach the farther side of the by-pass. The diversion of traffic from Chawton has surely, therefore, been a mixed blessing. The price has been the creeping 'urbanisation' of the village – there have also been the housing developments and the paving over of verges – and, to a great extent, its isolation from the surrounding countryside.

II. THE GREAT HOUSE

T HE COTTAGE BY THE POND, long converted from a posting-inn,
had been occupied before the Austens by one Bridger Seward, the
bailiff for the Chawton estate. The manor of Chawton, comprising,
at that time, the whole of the parish, had been made over to Jane's third
brother Edward in 1797, part of a dazzling gift which had included property
elsewhere in Hampshire (including their birthplace at Steventon) and at
Godmersham in Kent.

These estates had been consigned to Edward Austen in her lifetime by
the widowed Mrs Thomas Knight. The Knights, distant kinsfolk of the
Austens, were childless. With his parents' encouragement, they had begun
to treat the young Edward as their adopted son. They had had him to stay
with them during the summer holidays, sent him, in due course, on the
'Grand Tour', and eventually had appointed him the sole heir to both their
name and their property.

Thomas Knight's father, a Brodnax of Godmersham, had himself
inherited Chawton from a cousin, Elizabeth Knight (formerly Martin). This
imperious and bountiful lady, whose visits here used to be celebrated with a
peal of bells, had been the nearest surviving relative and heiress of Sir

Richard Knight, last of the Knights of Chawton, who had died in 1679. The name of Chawton's original owners had been adopted by the Martins and Brodnaxes who succeeded them as a condition of their inheritance. The same proviso was to be observed, following the death of his benefactress in 1812, by a grateful Edward Austen.

Despite the ultimate failure of their line, the original Knights of Chawton (with whom the Austens had no blood connection whatever) had been a conspicuously successful family. The Knights were descended from peasant stock, and their name is a particularly common one in Hampshire. They had been tenants of the manor of Chawton since at least the early 14th century (a 'John le Knight' appears in documents of 1323 and 1334 and a 'Walter Knyght' is mentioned in 1387), retaining and no doubt augmenting the same core holding of lands. During the 16th century, throughout which time the head of the family was content to describe himself as a 'yeoman' or 'farmer', they had acquired in turn a lease of the manor, the freehold of the family farm, and, in 1578, the lordship of Chawton itself, having cultivated cordial relations with their absentee landlords.

The acquisition of the lordship by the Knight family was promptly marked by the construction, in flint, of a new manor-house at Chawton, probably on the exact site of its medieval predecessor. (This is suggested by the orientation of the new building, its living rooms facing uncomfortably to the west and north.) Work on the house, commissioned by John Knight soon after his accession in 1585, was still in progress a short time before his death in 1620. It was evidently his life's passion. **Chawton House** – the 'Great House' – is at the southern end of the village, on a hillside above the **Church**. It is not open to the public, but the **west front**, still much as John Knight would have known it, can be viewed at close quarters from the gate. Both the house and the church are reached by the **carriage-drive**, a public footpath only, which connects them to the old Gosport Road.

The position of the **entrance porch**, on the extreme right-hand side of the building, is unusual. It is as if an additional wing were needed to complete the classic E-shaped design. To the left of the main entrance, built above vaulted brick cellars, is the Great Hall. Such rooms are medieval institutions, and were originally intended for communal activity, including feasts. In more modern times, it has been used as a drawing-room. Typically, the Great Hall at Chawton is entered, from a passage, through the two openings in an ancient oak screen - it may once have supported a gallery over the passage - which is probably Elizabethan in date and not, as previously suggested, a relic of the medieval building. (It is possible, however, that a disused fireplace in the wood cupboard was part of the medieval kitchen, and another, discovered on the north wall in 2001, may be of similar date.) There is oak panelling throughout, to the height of two thirds of each wall, much of it richly carved, which according to tree-ring tests may have been fitted as late as the 1620s. There is also a flat plaster ceiling which is believed to be original.

Opposite the two large mullioned windows which light the room is a splendid fireplace, backed by herring-bone brickwork. A decorative fireback bears the initials of John Knight and a date, 1588, perhaps the year in which this room was completed. In the same year, incidentally, John contributed generously to the defence of England against the Spanish Armada.

Beyond the Great Hall, the Great Staircase leads sumptuously to the Tapestry Gallery and East Gallery above. Each of these connecting rooms is panelled and has its original fireplace in the east wall. It appears that there was once a dog-gate at the top of the stairs. Adjacent to the Great Staircase, on the ground-floor of the north-west wing, is the Dining Room, whose original panelling survived until the early 19th century, and was skilfully replaced, some decades later, by the estate carpenter. Latterly, the portraits of Mr and Mrs Thomas Knight by Romney were hung here. It is on record that the bedrooms above were newly fitted out by John Knight in 1614.

John's great-nephew and eventual heir, Richard Knight, is credited with dramatic extensions to the house, including the stone-floored kitchen at the rear (north-east side) of the building, with a chamber above, and the red-brick wing, with its additional two gables, which forms the greater part of the present **south front.** It has long been in doubt whether Richard, a minor at the time, could have commissioned the two rear wings of the house. Recent tree-ring tests have settled the argument, as they show that the timbers here were felled in the winter of 1654-5. Furthermore, they reveal that the north-east wing was re-roofed in about 1666. The kitchen, which faces onto a courtyard, has been unaltered since Victorian times (a more modern one having been installed nearby), and retains its 'Flavell' range, chopping block and other remarkable features from the past.

The south front includes, at the end nearest the main entrance, the study or parlour (formerly a buttery), a room which is actually mentioned in John Knight's accounts from 1597. Beyond it is a hall containing the magnificent south stairway. At the opposite (south-west) end of this wing is the Library, at one time a Drawing Room. It is in this, one of the lightest and most comfortable rooms in the house, that the Lewkenor Carpet was hung. An heraldic tapestry, measuring some 16 feet by 7 feet, the Carpet was perhaps Chawton's greatest treasure. It was executed in 1564, probably in France, and was brought here from West Dean, the Lewkenor seat in Sussex, by Thomas Brodnax. Sold by the last resident squire, it is now in the Metropolitan Museum of Art in Washington, D.C., but is in too fragile a condition to be exhibited. One of the upstairs rooms in this wing is the Long Gallery; a carved door-head, inscribed 'R.K. 1655', is the firmest evidence of Richard Knight's involvement. The door-case in question, described as being 'in a class entirely of its own', has been moved twice in the last hundred years and now faces the main staircase.

King Charles I may well have passed through Chawton on 20 December 1648. His journey had begun on the Isle of Wight and was to end on the scaffold at Whitehall. Perhaps the young Richard Knight and his mother had seen him riding by with his escort. Knighted in his twenties, Richard was to die, childless, before the age of 40. He had been determined, however, to preserve the memory of his family. The sum of £500, set aside for the purpose in his will, assured him of a splendid monument in Chawton Church, whilst the adoption of his surname was a strict condition that he imposed on each of his successors, the most immediate of whom were the offspring of his first cousin, Michael Martin.

Of these, Elizabeth Knight (born Martin), who succeeded in 1702, was also the lady of West Dean, in Sussex, as heiress to the Lewkenor family. She was often in residence at Chawton, however. The cement coating, painted white, which was to adorn the exterior of the manor-house into Jane Austen's day and beyond, was no doubt one of Elizabeth's 'improvements'. A painting from this period shows there also to have been a formal terraced garden at the front of the house, enclosed by a fence, through which steps descended down to a gate at the level of the church. At the time of the painting, the hedge which fenced this garden was surmounted by topiary work representing running foxes and hounds. There is evidence to suggest the presence of formal gardens on this site since at least 1350.

Elizabeth Knight died in 1737, twice married, but childless. The Godmersham Knights, who reigned after her, were absentees. Sixty years later, the Chawton House that was passed on to Edward Austen was therefore in a 'somewhat dilapidated state', and he, too, favoured Godmersham (whose mansion-house was considerably finer, and more modern) as a residence. Chawton continued to be let to a series of short-term tenants, persons of fortune such as Mr Bingley in *Pride and Prejudice*, whose arrival at Netherfield Park was the cause of such excitement in the

Bennet household. Edward was only occasionally in residence himself, during the intervals between tenancies. For other members of the Austen family, including Jane, the first opportunity to become acquainted with Chawton was a ten-day house party which Edward hosted there in September 1807.

Edward's daughter Fanny, who became a great favourite of her aunt Jane, was to describe the pleasure of discovering the venerable old house: 'here are such a number of old irregular passages &c &c that it is very entertaining to explore them, & often when I think myself miles away from one part of the house I find a passage or entrance close to it, & I don't know when I shall be quite mistress of all the intricate, & different ways. It is very curious to trace the genealogy of the Knights & all the old families that have possessed this estate, from the pictures of which there are quantities, & some descriptions of them have been routed out, so that we are not at a loss for amusement.'

By the time, two years later, that Jane and the other Austen ladies had installed themselves in the corner cottage, the 'Great House', as it was always known, was again in the possession of a tenant. Edward was able to stay there for only three weeks in April 1812; but he moved his entire household to Chawton for the summer of 1813, whilst Godmersham was being refurbished. Jane, a regular visitor, had the opportunity to pass many 'a delicious morning' with Fanny, her affectionate niece. Edward and his family returned for a further two months in the summer of 1814, and thereafter, until the time when his eldest son decided to take up residence there, the house was reserved for the use of his sailor brothers, the future admirals Charles and Frank, during their runs ashore. It is believed that Frank's son Herbert was, in 1815, the first child to be born in the house since the 17th century.

Edward was a keen improver of the landscape. He had inherited a garden which was to be described by Jane as 'a bad one and ill situated', for it was in what is now the **meadow** between the church and the old Gosport road. In the summer of 1813, Jane writes of his intention to make a new one, 'at the top of the Lawn behind his own house'. Elizabeth Knight's walled enclosure, at the front of the house, was (or had already been) dismantled. At the rear of the building, steps had led up from a forecourt to a garden terrace, set with formal 'squares', and there had originally been an orchard and a bowling alley on the hill above. Edward built on a conservatory, from which a winding path led instead to flower beds and a kitchen garden. As anticipated by Jane, a larger walled garden was laid on the top terrace, probably at the expense of a little temple (shown in a contemporary painting) in which she is said, somewhat improbably, to have written. Other formal features, on the south side, were replaced with rolling lawns.

Edward was also responsible, apparently, for the greater parkland beyond, which now is such an attractive feature of the estate. Most of this land is known to have been under the plough until at least 1811, when the landscaped area around the house had been restricted to a mere 19 acres. Whether Jane Austen lived to see much of her brother's alterations is a matter of doubt. Many of the trees, for example, were planted in 1821–2, some time after her death. Chawton House is often credited with being the model for Donwell Abbey in *Emma* (begun in 1814), whilst its gardens perhaps appear in *Mansfield Park* (written between 1811 and 1813). However, if any real places inspired the scenes of Jane's novels, it is impossible to identify them from her physical descriptions, which are notoriously, and no doubt purposefully, vague.

Jane's nephew, Edward Knight (1794–1879), 'an intelligent and keen sportsman and an unrivalled horseman', took up permanent residence at Chawton in 1826. (Godmersham Park, a preference for which was maintained by the elder Edward until his death in 1852, was to be sold in 1874.) He added a block which, somewhat infelicitously, abutted the **north-west wall** of the old house, containing a billiard room with bedrooms above. He also constructed a new servants' wing at the back of the house. Regarded as liabilities, these extensions were demolished in 1999. Edward had no doubt had need of this extra space, for he kept a considerable establishment. At the Census taken on 30 April 1861, his household consisted of no less than 37 people. As well as his wife, and eight of his sixteen children, four of their Portal relatives were paying a visit. The staff consisted of a governess, a butler, two footmen, a coachman, two grooms, a gardener, a housekeeper, two lady's maids, a nurse, two nurse maids, three laundry maids, a dairy maid, two house maids, a kitchen maid, a scullery maid and a still room maid!

The son who succeeded him, Montagu George Knight (born in 1844, and educated at Eton and Oxford) was to strip away the 18th-century stucco, and to replace the later sash windows with mullioned ones, in an attempt to re-create the original appearance of the house. The results of his work, which he undertook some time after 1903, are considered by some to be unpleasing. A generous, public-spirited and benevolent squire of the old school, Montagu Knight died in 1914, leaving no issue. As has been accurately pointed out, 'things in the village were never to be quite the same ever again'.

The disintegration of Chawton Manor, and the collapse of its centuries-old way of life, began in 1919, with the sale of 220 outlying acres. In 1921, much of the northern part of the estate was also sold. The lots included **Truncheant's Farm** (originally purchased by Nicholas Knight in 1583), and a number of houses opening onto the **Butts**. Lt-Col. Lionel Knight (1872–1931), Montagu's nephew, had returned from the war to live at Chawton, but had found himself unable to preserve his inheritance. The Colonel's son, Major Edward Knight (1910–1987), was obliged to make further sacrifices. It was he who relinquished, in 1951, the major part of the village of Chawton, consisting of the freehold of 34 cottages and gardens, together with that of the 'Grey Friar' Inn.

The family had parted with the remaining portions of the estate by 1989, when Major Knight's son Richard (born in 1940), left with a crumbling mansion but without enough land to sustain it, agreed to sell the 'Great House' itself - albeit on a 125-year lease - to a group of businessmen. Their failure to raise the £1,300,000 purchase price spared Chawton House from an undignified future. Instead, the lease was acquired in 1993 by Ms Sandy Lerner, an American philanthropist, who, with the approval and active support of the Knight family, has restored the house and grounds. Open to students from July 2003, Chawton House now serves as a 'Centre for the Study of Early English Women's Writing' - an elegant and imaginative solution to Mr Knight's predicament.

III. THE LAW OF THE FOREST

LORDSHIPS OF THE MANOR were a medieval relic which, by legislation of 1925, had ceased to have any practical significance. For the best part of a millennium beforehand, however, all life in Chawton had been subject, in some degree, to the authority of its lord. Successive lords of the manor, autocratic, neglectful, and benevolent by turns, have shaped the Chawton that we know today.

The earliest reference to Chawton is in *Domesday Book*, from 1086. The settlement that the Saxons called 'Cealfa-tun', from the calves that were reared there, would have been no more than a clearing in an all-embracing expanse of forest; but the Romans may earlier have created a villa estate at Chawton, in the days when Neatham, now a tiny hamlet on the north-east side of Alton, was a flourishing town.

Chawton's owner at the time of the Norman Conquest, a Saxon thane called Oda of Winchester, had survived an upheaval in which most of his peers were dispossessed, killed or exiled. Perhaps he was a turncoat. The *Domesday* evidence suggests that Oda's Chawton was a collection of scattered homesteads; its 33 householders must have scratched out a somewhat precarious living, although they enjoyed extensive rights to graze their pigs in the surrounding woodland.

The Norman kings, however, were passionate sportsmen, and brooked the minimum of encroachment on the still-extensive forests of England. The hated 'Forest Law' was therefore applied here, in parallel with all other forms of jurisdiction. Hunting for deer or wild boar was forbidden to all but the king and his favourites, on pain of horrible punishment; so, too, was any activity that disturbed their habitat, such as cutting trees. In about 1087, William the Conqueror granted Chawton to a Norman ally, Hugh de Port, Oda being obliged to accept other lands in exchange. Hugh's descendants, who adopted the surname of their maternal ancestors, the St Johns, must have had special permission to cut great swathes into the woodland and plough them up – as happened also on their estate at Sherborne St John – thereby imposing on Chawton the familiar characteristics of a medieval English manor.

Under the authority of the St Johns, the peasantry of Chawton was organised into a co-operative farming community. The open fields that had been created on both sides of the Gosport Road were to be cultivated by group effort and according to a common policy. The holding that was allocated to each tenant, which amounted to between four and sixteen acres, was distributed across the common fields in a scattering of 1½-acre strips. Unusually, the villagers appear to have ground their corn in a windmill (the technology for which is said to have been brought back from the East by Richard the Lionheart), since the **Lavant stream**, which flows through Chawton, has a tendency to run dry, and would have been inadequate to power a watermill. The site of this windmill used to be marked by '**Windmill Field**', to the east of Chawton House. **Chawton Common**, 321 acres in the west of the parish, bordering Chawton Park Wood, was the common hayfield and pasturage.

A residence was maintained at Chawton from at least 1224. The manor-house that was constructed in that year by William de St John included a pair of oaks from the nearby Alice Holt Forest, a gift from the King. However, the mighty St John barony was dispersed across six counties, and composed of dozens of similar manors. (The remains of their stronghold at Basing, in the north of Hampshire, can still be seen.) The lord might regularly tour his various properties, but his stay in each place would usually be brief. As typical barons, the St Johns devoted much of their time to the service of the king, whether as counsellors and companions or in prominent military and administrative roles. The privileges they received in return are an indication of their favoured status at court.

William's son Robert procured, in 1252, an immunity from the Forest Law on his own land at Chawton: Henry III had consented to his hunting freely there. The family were permitted, moreover, to create a private hunting reserve, and to enclose it with a sunken fence, or 'leap', to prevent the deer from straying. The memory of Chawton Park, with its 1,000-acre 'Great Park' and 100-acre 'Little Park' (which are presumed to have been adjacent), is preserved not only in its name. Much of the surrounding deer leap or '**Pale**', undisturbed ever since, is still an impressive sight, especially at the Medstead and Beech ends of the Park.

The monarchy may well have encouraged these improvements in land use at Chawton, and to its sporting facilities, out of self interest. With a vast empire to oversee (it extended from Scotland to the Pyrenees) and little time to spend in any one place, the Angevin kings used, in the 13th century, regularly to descend on Chawton for a night or two, finding it a convenient place to break the journey between their castles at Guildford and Winchester. During those brief periods, the country would actually be governed from Chawton. Only an efficiently organised manor could have catered for the prodigious appetites of the royal household, scores of knights, clerks and valets who would presumably have eaten and slept communally in the Great Hall of the manor-house. For the King, the opportunity to hunt here for fresh meat would have been an added attraction.

These royal visits must have imposed a heavy burden on the peasantry, although the Lord of St John was not himself expected to bear the costs. Robert's son John, a 'most faithful and valiant knight', was a close associate of Edward I, and accompanied him, before his accession, on his Crusade to the Holy Land (1270–72): there may well have been one or two Chawton men in their train. Later, as a *banneret* (or military commander) he participated in the conquest of Wales, before serving as Lieutenant of Edward's duchy of Aquitaine. As such, he was taken prisoner in 1297 in an action against the French (who are said to have rejoiced over his capture 'as the Philistines rejoiced over that of Samson'), brought in triumph to Paris, and held ruinously to ransom for eighteen months. On his return, he was immediately given a commission in the war against the Scots. A minstrel with a keen eye for heraldry was to celebrate 'the brave John de St John', who, at the Siege of Carlaverock in 1300, 'was everywhere with Edward, Prince of Wales, and on his white caparisons had upon a red chief two gold mullets [stars]'.

As the medieval equivalent of a multi-millionaire, a man like John de St John was expected to make a conspicuous show of his rank and wealth. The chivalric virtue that would have endeared him most to his tenants was that of *largesse*, or open-handed generosity. Whether 'free' or 'servile', they would originally have paid for their holdings at Chawton with their labour. All would have been obliged, at certain periods, to work on the allotments of the lord (more numerous, of course, than their own), on top of the back-breaking task of providing for themselves. Unlike the freemen, of whom, soon after John's death in 1301, there were eight, the twenty-two serfs at Chawton were technically at the lord's permanent disposal. However, the amount of time which even the serfs would have to work 'for the lord's food' had, by that date, been limited to a few weeks in the year. In common with other 14th-century landowners, the Lord of St John had preferred to receive payment from his tenants in cash, along with regular dues from each of them such as a cock and a hen. In 1302, these were demanded also from the four smallholding 'cottagers' who lived at Chawton, poor as they were. A couple of the freemen paid their rent in the form of arrowheads – probably those with an interest in the fields called 'Arrow Croft' and 'Orchards', the latter name a corrupted form of 'Archers'.

The St Johns do not seem to have inspired much loyalty among the locals. While John was away in Gascony, his deer were freely poached. In 1333, during the reign of Hugh, John's son, Chawton Park was to be trespassed upon by a group of hunting clergy, the parson of nearby Shalden among them. (The ubiquitous clergy of those days included many who had convictions for poaching.) A more dramatic development followed in 1338, when King Edward III, guardian to Hugh's heir, a minor, ordered the arrest and imprisonment of almost every prominent inhabitant of Chawton. Suspected of pilfering manorial property, they included the village chaplain, Thomas the Summoner, and Nicholas, the park-keeper, the man who was presumably expected to ward off, rather than to encourage the poachers. As we have already seen, Chawton was not exempt from the general lawlessness, and even violence, of medieval England.

Following the extinction, in 1361, of the St John line, the estate was to pass through heiresses into the Poynings, Bonville and West families. The old manor-house, once the haunt of kings, was neglected, and perhaps abandoned. Virtually nothing is known of the early building: its very position is uncertain. When the Knights acquired their lease of the 'cite' in 1524, the manorial rents were still being paid there. There are strong suggestions that at least part of the medieval building had survived and that it was incorporated into the present Chawton House. Family tradition has it that the old house was fronted by a moat, on the side facing the church, and that this was laboriously filled in by John Knight when embarking on his reconstruction. He may also have adopted what remained of the two medieval gardens. But the Chantry Chapel of St Laurence, founded within the manor, some time before 1245, by Robert de St John, had been converted to other uses by the time of the Dissolution of the Monasteries – assuming that the building had survived at all.

Whilst the lordship had declined, the tenants had prospered, their rights of succession protected under customary law. In 1320, Hugh Bean, one of the freemen who had paid his rent in arrowheads, was confirmed in his four-acre holding in the north of the parish. It was between the Pass of Alton and 'Mundchamesrude' – an early rendering, perhaps, of 'Mounter's Lane'. The Beans were still farming the open fields at Chawton, communally with their neighbours, in the reign of Elizabeth I. Such families may later have died out or moved away: by the beginning of the 18th century, Barret, Croucher and Morey, names prominent in Tudor Chawton, had yielded to Prowting, Harris and Eames. The Alderslades and the Dawes had survived, but they, too, were soon to disappear. The landscape, however, including much of the woodland that had, from early times, surrounded the village, was unaffected by these changes. That transformation was to occur in 1741, when, with local approval, an Enclosure Act was passed, enabling the land to be re-distributed and cultivated in a more efficient manner. The thirty 'commoners' of 1302 had been reduced by this date to a mere nine (including a couple of charitable institutions). This evidence suggests that, whilst many of the holdings may have been combined as a result of intermarriage, the thriftier tenants, like the Knights, can only have benefited over time from the failings of their neighbours.

IV. THE PASS OF ALTON

IT IS DIFFICULT to think of the pathway through Chawton Park Wood as a once busy thoroughfare, or, indeed, as a den of thieves. To Jane Austen and her contemporaries, the course of the former highway was still apparent. The broad corridor which it formed along the southern edge of the Park is clearly shown on the Tithe Map of 1840. Although described as 'Chawton Lower Common', it corresponds exactly with the 'Road from Alresford to Alton' as marked on an estate map of 1741.

The site of the Pass of Alton, known as such until at least the 17th century, is now marked by a footpath designated the 'Peter Wykeham Way'. Chawton Park Road, into which it merges, east of the Park, is merely the modern manifestation of the old 'Paceway Road', as it was still called in the early part of the 20th century. (There was also a 'Peace-Way Close' nearby.) Happily, the name of this place outlived its notoriety.

In the 13th and 14th centuries, criminal activity on the Pass was the cause of deep concern to successive kings. It perhaps owed its proverbial bad name to one incident more than any other. In the autumn of 1248, a pair of Brabantine merchants was attacked on the Pass by 'freebooters' and robbed of 200 marks, a very considerable sum (and weight) of money. Their plight came to the attention of King Henry III, who immediately ordered a judicial enquiry. It soon emerged that the robbing of the merchants had been part of a much wider criminal conspiracy, in which members of the local gentry, and even of the royal household, were implicated.

Some of the suspects were brought to trial on 14 January 1249, but were acquitted by a jury consisting of their own friends and neighbours. The King, who was in Winchester shortly afterwards, was appalled. He summoned the suspected abettors of the crime to his presence in the Great Hall. Twelve of them were elected to a second jury, and sworn to give up the names of the criminals. By refusing to reveal any information, they were considered to have perjured themselves and were condemned to be hanged.

A third jury decided, after some initial hesitation, to co-operate. Their disclosures about dozens of crimes that had been committed throughout the county, many of the culprits being persons of wealth and position, were sensational. In connection with the robbery of the merchants, no less than sixty-four men and women were to be charged as a result, either as principals or accessories. At least nine of them were subsequently hanged.

As the contemporary chronicler Matthew Paris puts it, 'Winchester, Southampton, and the whole of that county incurred an indelible stain of infamy and opprobrium from these occurrences'. He hoped that the fate of those convicted would deter such villainy in the future. On the contrary, highway robbery on the Pass continued to be a flourishing local industry for a century or more. Edward I and his barons may have had it in mind when, in 1285, they enacted the famous *Statute of Winchester*. 'From day to day robberies, homicides and arsons are more often committed than they used to be,' ran the preamble. Crimes were generally being condoned, juries were corrupt, and, indeed, it was thought to be no crime at all to rob a stranger, or to receive the property stolen from him. Edward, of course, knew the area well, from his frequent visits to Chawton Manor. He would have remembered the attack on the royal baggage-train that had taken place in 1261. It may have been here, too, that he had had his reckoning with Sir Adam de Gurdon in 1266. A leading participant in the rebellion of Simon de Montfort, who had been disinherited after its defeat, Sir Adam had retreated to a fastness in 'Alton Wood'. From here, he had 'raided the countryside, particularly the lands of those who adhered to the royal cause'. Edward had hunted him down and engaged him in single combat, but had pardoned him on account of his valour, and had restored him, subsequently, to his estates at Selborne and East Tisted.

The Statute of Winchester was to provide for the widening of such roads as the Pass, to ensure that there was no cover for the would-be highwayman. Whatever measures may have been taken here, the Pass was still considered, in the 14th century, to be unsafe. The wardens of the annual Great Fair of St Giles at Winchester had kept up their practice of posting five mounted sergeants on the Pass for its duration. Langland's reference to it in *Piers Plowman*, which dates from the end of the century, is a further measure of its infamy. Clearly, the best efforts of central and local authority during the past two centuries had failed to achieve any solution to this pressing problem.

Robberies on the Pass of Alton were a protracted problem because they were condoned by the local inhabitants. (The jurors at the third trial in 1249 had included a John de Chawton and a Henry Wyard: '**Wyard's Farm**' exists to this day, at Beech, on the northern side of Chawton Park, and its farmhouse, rebuilt in 1691, was the home of Jane Austen's niece Anna Lefroy from 1815.) As we have already seen, there is ample evidence of their criminal tendencies, such as the arrest, in 1338, of almost all the prominent people in Chawton. The medieval residents of the parish were, quite simply, opportunistic thieves. Whilst their disdain for the King and their lord is evident, their crimes could hardly be justified as blows against authority. From the stolen goods that were recovered after the robbery of 1248, it is clear that the participants had been motivated by sheer greed for the rich pickings that were available, rather than from any higher impulse. In the 13th century, and perhaps beyond, the lord of St John had maintained a gallows beside the old road, the site of which is marked to this day by '**Gibbet Copse**'. The honest traveller may have been lulled by it into a false sense of security. For the medieval highwaymen on the Pass, though, the deterrent effect would appear to have been minimal.

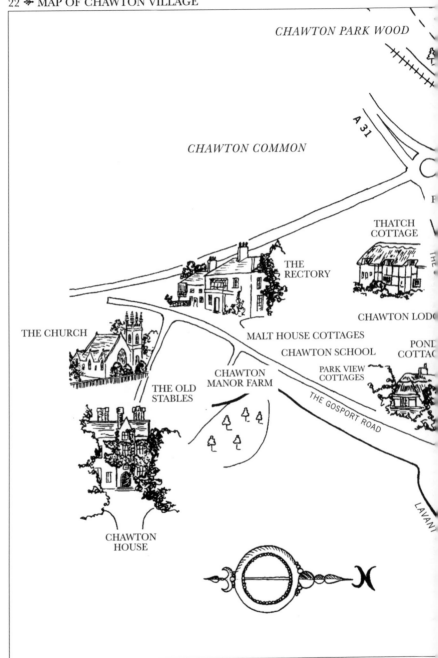

CHAWTON PARK WOOD

A 31

CHAWTON COMMON

THATCH
COTTAGE

THE
RECTORY

CHAWTON LODG

THE CHURCH

MALT HOUSE COTTAGES

CHAWTON SCHOOL

POND
COTTAG

THE OLD
STABLES

CHAWTON
MANOR FARM

PARK VIEW
COTTAGES

THE GOSPORT ROAD

LAVAN

CHAWTON
HOUSE

the Knight family in their hey-day: there was accommodation at the rear for no less than five horse-drawn carriages. There is also a large coach-house at the back, which would have been the living quarters for the coachmen and grooms.

In 1982, the stable block was sold by Major Edward Knight to developers. The main building was stripped of its 19th-century stalls and other original features and converted into a single dwelling with seven bedrooms, three bathrooms and four reception rooms. The property was offered for sale again in 1988 at a price of £600,000. It has since been acquired by Ms Lerner.

To the rear of the old stables is **CHAWTON MANOR FARM** – the Home Farm. It is reached by a private lane which peels off from the Gosport Road at the **Pasture Gate**, opposite the **Malt House Cottages**. This, in fact, is the old coach road to Chawton House. The farmhouse is a handsome brick building, essentially of the early 17th century, but with mid-19th-century alterations. There is a **brewhouse** at one end, and beyond it a large, probably late-Tudor **dovecote,** long-abandoned. Another nearby building, now called **THE DOVECOTE,** was probably not designed as such, for there are no nesting ledges, but may have served as a kennel for hunting dogs or as a falconry mews. At any rate it was built at about the same time as the Old Stables, 'of similar materials and with the same quality of decoration, making it a small building of some architectural pretension'. It has recently been converted into a dwelling, as has an adjacent barn.

Directly opposite the old Stables is the parish **CHURCH**. In its present state, this would not have been recognised by Jane Austen. She worshipped in a simple, and apparently rather dilapidated building on the same site. First documented in 1291, it consisted of a nave and a chancel, with a tower at the western end. The original entrance, shown in an early 18th-century painting, was in the middle of the north wall of the nave, and was enclosed by a porch. The church next appears in a painting of 1809. The porch had disappeared by this date, the tower had been rebuilt, and a new entrance had been made in the centre of the western end, the design of which, by no coincidence, bore a startling resemblance to that at Steventon.

The Austen ladies would take their regular seats on the south side of the aisle, where the women of the parish were segregated. Places in the high, boxed pews of those days – these had been installed by Elizabeth Knight and her second husband, Bulstrode Peachey, in 1733 – were strictly allotted. Behind them, at the western end, was a gallery, which provided extra accommodation for some of the humbler parishioners.

The chancel was separated from the nave in Jane's day by an unusual screen in the form of a wall. This had been plastered over, no doubt at the Reformation. Jane could not have known, then, that the surface beneath was 'covered all over with paintings, apparently figures of persons', nor have guessed that the entire medieval church might once have been decorated in this way.

Unfortunately, these precious relics from the past seem to have been little appreciated by Jane's family. In 1838 the Squire and his son, who had recently been appointed Rector, were content to demolish the entire western end of the building, and to rebuild, on the same foundations, in charmless brick. Only the medieval chancel was preserved. (The Knight family vault beneath was later to be restored.) In their eagerness to be rid of the decaying structure, the historic screen was blithely sacrificed. Jane Austen's sister Cassandra had generously contributed £100 towards these operations.

The new building, with its plain windows, was of such ugliness that it was entirely encased in stucco. It might have been with us still, had a fire not broken out in 1871 (caused by a faulty heating system, newly installed), which almost completely gutted the nave. The pews of 1733 were a regrettable loss: only the memorial tablets at the eastern end, including those to Jane Austen's mother and sister, were salvaged.

The present building, swiftly resurrected on the site, was designed by Arthur Blomfield, the fashionable London architect (later knighted) who had earlier employed the young Thomas Hardy as a draughtsman. Blomfield's church is a satisfying blend of red sandstone and flint, and is entered, like its predecessor, through a porch at the south-western corner.

The chief glory within is the monument to Sir Richard Knight (died 1679), for which he had made such careful provision in his will. His marble effigy, a reclining figure in armour, is a major work by the Oxford mason William Byrd. The yeoman Knights had clearly come a long way, but Sir Richard, sadly, was the last of his line. The monument is in the chancel and was therefore immune from all the subsequent damage to the nave. The chancel has, however, been restored to such a degree that it is no longer recognisably medieval.

The **CARRIAGE DRIVE** was probably created in the middle of the 19th century. It does not appear in the early 18th-century painting of Chawton Manor, and the centenarian John White, who was born in 1821, remembered the old road from the Pasture Gate, opposite the Malt House Cottages, being used in his youth. The old road leads up to a gate at the back of the Great House, where there are additional stables and outhouses. These also seem to date from the 19th century, by which time the Elizabethan stable block was presumably considered redundant.

Opposite the entrance to the carriage drive, on the farther side of the Gosport Road, is the former **RECTORY**. This was re-built in 1803, within a year of his appointment, by the Rev. John Rawstorn Papillon (1763–1837), who also made improvements to the surrounding glebeland. The names of the Rectors are known since 1289, and a painting of the previous Rectory, now in the Jane Austen Museum, shows a dignified, 17th-century façade. Papillon was a connection of the Godmersham Knights. A bachelor, he lived here with his unmarried sister, Elizabeth. Mrs Thomas Knight had suggested in 1809 that Mr Papillon would make a suitable husband for Jane, and this had become a family joke. Jane had a good deal to do with them nonetheless, and refers to Elizabeth as being 'handsome'. Papillon, whose name was pronounced 'Pillion' by the locals, was succeeded in 1837 by one of Jane's nephews, the Rev. Charles Bridges Knight.

Further along the Gosport Road, in the direction of the village, **CHAWTON SCHOOL**, now a Church of England primary school, was originally founded in 1840 by Mr Edward Knight. It was for children of both sexes, and was run by a mistress with the assistance of a pupil-teacher. The present schoolhouse was erected in 1882 by Mr Montagu Knight. The Victorian building has been regularly refurbished since, most recently in 1993, and a substantial new wing was added in 2002. A Chawton school had previously been kept elsewhere in the village, the children being 'only taught some reading'. This was said in 1788 to have been 'supported chiefly by the annual bounty of Thomas Knight Esq.'

The **POND COTTAGES** beyond, near the corner where there was once a pond, are perhaps the oldest dwellings in Chawton. The 'cruck' frames that support them – massive timbers, bent into arches at either end – are typical of the late Middle Ages. Elsewhere in Hampshire, a number of similar buildings have been scientifically dated to this period.

Turning left into the Winchester Road, one comes immediately upon **CHAWTON LODGE**. An attractive building thought to date from the 1760s, it seems to have been altered little since Jane's time. Formerly part of the copyhold estate of James Alderslade, the house, with attached orchard and garden, was acquired in 1802 by Miss Jane Hinton, then aged 28. She was to marry the Rev. Dr. James Ventris in 1816, having shared the house with her (twin?) brother, John Knight Hinton (1774 - 1846), known as 'Jack'. They were the children of a previous Rector (who had also lived here briefly before his death in 1802), and the family were the last true descendants of the original Knights of Chawton. Understandably enough, they regarded the Austen family as intruders. Pointing out that the estate had been entailed to them under the will of old Elizabeth Knight, and citing 'some informality in a disentailing deed of 1758', they were to issue proceeedings against Jane Austen's brother Edward in 1814, seeking to eject him from the property. Relations with their neighbours across the road must have been considerably strained as a result, although the Hintons' nephew James Baverstock, 'a clever and rather scampish brewer of Alton', was identified as the instigator of the dispute. The matter was finally settled in 1818 by a payment to the Hintons of £15,000. The money was raised by the sale of timber from Chawton Park Wood, creating a scar in the wood which is visible to this day. The two families had presumably been reconciled by 1836, when the Knights accepted £200 from Dr Ventris for the freehold. He died in 1841, aged 80, his widow staying on in the house until her own death in 1856, aged 85. Later residents have included (1899-1926) Walter Harries Pollock, the literary critic, who entertained Sir Henry Irving here, and a Miss Lowenthal (1970-75), who commissioned John Fowler, founder of Colefax and Fowler, to re-design the garden.

The neighbouring **THATCH COTTAGE** was, until its award-winning restoration in modern times, some of the poorest housing in Chawton. It is thought to be a mainly Tudor building, but there is a mid-18th-century addition on the east end. Described as a house and shop, set in an acre of land, the property was held by the Harris family until 1758, when it was acquired by Edward Philmore, a carpenter. Edward was succeeded in 1786 by his son John, the 'Old Philmore' of Jane Austen's letters.

Through most of the nineteenth century, the building was divided into two - the separate staircases are still intact - and there is evidence that such a division had occurred by the 1820s. There is a strong possibility, therefore, that one of these cottages had been the miserable quarters of Miss Mary Benn, an indigent gentlewoman, to whom Jane Austen refers frequently in her letters. Mary Benn's brother was the Rector of nearby Farringdon, but he had a growing family of his own and was unable to accommodate her. Unsuitably housed, and lacking, at times, the services of a maid, Miss Benn was treated with great sympathy by the Austen ladies. They regularly received her at their cottage across the road for tea or dinner, although she was in no position ever to return their hospitality. Indeed, Miss Benn seems to have been treated with similar consideration by all the gentry of the village. A friend of Jane's who wished, in 1812, to make Mary a present was advised that 'something of the Shawl kind to wear over her Shoulders within doors in very cold weather might be useful, but it must not be very handsome or she would not use it'. In February 1813, Jane writes of Miss Benn's 'wretched abode' that it had been 'terrible for her in the late storms of wind & rain'. Evicted in that year by her landlord, 'Old Philmore', in favour of his son, the unfortunate Miss Benn ended up in lodgings, although Jane hoped that 'they may not be long necessary'. She died during Christmas 1815, aged 46, and is buried in the churchyard. Her grave is unmarked.

Old Philmore's own funeral, in March 1817, is described as 'very handsome', with Triggs, the Chawton gamekeeper, 'walking behind in his Green Coat. Mrs Philmore attended as chief Mourner, in Bombasin, made very short, and flounced with Crape.' John's son Edward, aged 55, was duly admitted to the property, though part or all of it was soon being tenanted by members of the Gibbs family.

By the late 1820s, the village school was kept in the easternmost of the Thatch Cottages, Mrs Sarah Gibbs, a labourer's wife, being the mistress. She offered basic reading, but not writing skills, although Cassandra Austen, Jane's sister, may have helped. According to John White, who remembered her, Cassandra 'took a great interest in young girls, and taught them reading, the catechism and sewing'. As we have seen, the Chawton school was formally established, in 1840, in purpose-built premises along the Gosport Road, where it remains to this day. Isaac and James Gibbs were the tenants in that year of the two Thatch Cottages. The family had continued in occupation under Edward Knight, to whom the property had reverted in 1834, upon the death of Edward Philmore.

During the first half of the 20th century, the greater part of the building was home to the Turner family. In 1951, when the house was offered for sale by the Knight estate, the Turner cottage included four bedrooms and both the staircases. The adjoining cottage, at the western end, had been reduced to a single bedroom, to which the unfortunate tenant gained access by means of a ladder.

The crumbling Thatch Cottage of living memory, with its disintegrating roof, closely matches the description of Miss Benn's hovel in Jane's letter. In 1974, the building was threatened with demolition by developers. Fortunately, the local authorities intervened, and the house was bought by a retired couple, Mr and Mrs Peter Gannon, who have lovingly restored it and made it their home. The main fireplace - no doubt the one on which Richard Harris was taxed in 1665 - has been opened up, and the ancient beams exposed. Some of these, curiously, were found to have nails, hooks and traces of pitch attached to them. It seems that Chawton Park was once a major supplier of timber to the navy. Tradition has it that the wood from the redundant ships would be sent back to Chawton for use in the construction of houses. However, architectural historians are inclined to reject such picturesque theories - which are rife in Hampshire - in the absence of any firm evidence. The timbers from broken-up ships are likely in any case to have been rotten, though the use of second-hand wood from other sources was undoubtedly a common practice. The parish has at least one authentic maritime connection: there has been a recent Royal Navy minesweeper named H.M.S. *Chawton*.

On the opposite side of the Winchester Road, at the western extremity of the village, **POUND FARM** represents what, historically, was one of the larger holdings on the manor. The solid, elegant farmhouse is thought to date from the period of William and Mary. It is almost exactly contemporary, therefore, with the Austen house. The property consisted, by the 19th century, of 200 acres, and seems to have been passed through a series of short-term tenants.

Its neighbour to the east, **BAIGENS**, was once a farmhouse too, but is considerably older. Baigens would not have been recognised in its present form by Jane Austen. The dilapidated house was acquired (leasehold) in 1841 by her nephew, Edward Knight, who restored it. The Victorian outer brickwork now conceals a timber-framed structure that dates back to the late 15th century.

The house and its 160-acre holding were known historically not as 'Baigens' but as 'Symond's Farm'. William Symonds of Winchester, who died in 1604, had left it to the Corporation of that city in trust, its future rents to be used for the benefit of Winchester's poor. The property was tenanted for many years (until the 1840s) by members of the Baigent family, after whom a copse in Chawton Park Wood is also named. During the whole of Jane Austen's lifetime, it belonged to William Baigent, Yeoman, latterly as joint tenant with his wife Jane. The couple held it from the Corporation by a series of renewable short-term leases. In 1814, the Baigents' 10-year-old son James went to trial at Winchester for stabbing another Chawton boy, Stephen Mersh, and was acquitted. Jane Austen refers in one of her letters (dated March 1814) to the 'Baigent business'. Her brother Edward appears to have had little sympathy for young James, considering him guilty of assault if not of attempted murder. Legal advice had been sought in confidence by Mr Wickham of Pound Farm, who 'is to be on the Grand Jury.

This business must hasten an Intimacy between his family & my Brother's.'

Briefly divided into separate dwellings, the two halves of Baigens were to be reunited during the tenancy of James Pritchard (the village schoolmaster from 1881 to 1919), who, in 1933, acquired the freehold. Pritchard's daughters were to live here until 1967. During renovations of the interior by their successors, Major and Mrs Derek Robson, much of the Victorian plaster was stripped away. A remarkable set of wall paintings, blackened by smoke, was discovered above the main fireplace. The paintings, in seven panels, include representations of a hare and a deer, and are extraordinarily vivid. They were restored in 1974, and have since been dated to between 1525 and 1575. Floral patterns have also been discovered on the adjacent wall. Almost as remarkable as the paintings is the splendid fireplace in the former kitchen.

The **ground between Baigens and the corner cottage**, now occupied by a modern dwelling, was once attached to the Austen property, as was a garden, part of the present **car park**, on the opposite side of the road. The section of the road that runs north from this corner, in the direction of Alton, is treated today as a continuation of the Winchester Road. Strictly speaking, it is the old *Gosport* road that is joined at this point. Since the construction, in 1971, of the by-pass, neither name has been particularly appropriate. It would be more accurate to refer to the main road through the village as the 'Street', which is how it was known in Jane Austen's time and, indeed, within living memory. As for the Winchester Road, there is a case, perhaps, for calling it the 'Shrave' once more.

The cottage on the north-east side of Jane Austen's house, which its owners have dated, perhaps too conservatively, to the middle of the 16th century, is called '**CLINKERS**', after the family which occupied it from the first half of the 19th century. The Clinkers were in business in the adjacent **FORGE**, as blacksmiths and wheelwrights, until the 1930s. One of the next-door **IVY COTTAGES** may have been the home of John White (born in 1790), who was presumably known to Jane Austen. (The houses are not named in the early censuses, so it is possible that he lived across the road in either **Merrivale** or **Humphrey Cottage**). Invalided out of the army after the Battle of Waterloo, and unfit for regular work thereafter, White was dependent on the support of his many children, whose education suffered as a result. Of these, John White the younger, born in 1821, became a farm labourer, and lived in one of the **Park View Cottages** on the Gosport Road. He died at the age of 99, leaving some brief but valuable reminiscences of old Chawton. John White senior was still living in 1851, and was described in that year as a Chelsea Pensioner.

According to Caroline Austen, Jane's niece, the ladies at the corner cottage were 'upon *friendly* but rather *distant* terms' with all their neighbours. To judge from her correspondence, this would accurately describe Jane's relations with the Prowting family. The former farmhouse known today as **PROWTINGS** is set back in spacious grounds from the Street, a little to the north of the Austen house. The elderly William Prowting, whom Jane knew, lived here with his wife and daughters.

Of yeoman origin, the family was one of the most prominent in Chawton. In 1665, a Rowland Prowting had been credited, for tax purposes, with four hearths. In 1670, Rowland and his son Thomas had acquired the joint tenancy of a holding at Stonehills, at the north end of the village. William Prowting (*c.* 1679 - *c.* 1732) had become a member of the Society of Apothecaries of London, and in 1722 had taken on a second William, son of Rowland, as an apprentice. The younger William (1708 - 94) had built up a considerable practice from his premises on the corner of Tower Street and Mincing Lane (where he lived above the shop), and had commissioned radical alterations to the building, for which he employed George Dance, R.A., a prominent City architect. (Dance's original plans for Prowting's London house are preserved at Sir John Soane's Museum. The new features included a stunning oval staircase at the back of the property, a large walk-in safe in the Parlour and a water closet.) Like his uncle, William Prowting was an active member of the Society of Apothecaries, serving as Master in 1775-6, and, for a number of years, as Treasurer of the Navy Stock, the Society having been, since 1703, the official supplier of drugs and medicines to the Navy. A full-length portrait of the stern, bewigged William by Lemuel Abbott (who also painted what is probably the best-known image of Nelson) still hangs in the Great Hall at the Apothecaries' Hall, commissioned, it is said, 'to perpetuate a character so worthy of imitation'. Regrettably, he never employed an architect of Dance's stature on the family property at Chawton. By the time of his death, however, their wealth and status were considerable. The third William Prowting (son of his younger brother John), born in about 1754, was a magistrate and a Deputy Lieutenant for Hampshire.

This William succeeded to the Stonehills tenement of his uncle (who produced only daughters), but had no doubt already settled at 'Prowtings', which he was the first of his family to occupy. The farmhouse here has been known by their name since at least the 1820s. However, it had been the home, for many centuries beforehand, of the Morey family and of their heirs, the Fishers. The estate, formerly that of John Nevill of Broughton, seems to have been acquired by Richard Morey in 1367. A Thomas Morey who died in 1503 had directed that prayers should be said for himself and for other members of his family in the parish church. Another Thomas, the last of the direct line, had been killed at Lostwithiel in the Civil War, fighting on the side of the King. Thomas Morey had been succeeded by his infant daughter Ann, who, in 1660, had married William Fisher. At the enclosure of the common fields in 1741, the lands allotted to Ann's grandson, Forbes Fisher, had included Southfield and Wood Barn Farms, in the south and west of the parish. The present 'Prowtings' is also clearly marked, on an estate map of that year, as Mr Fisher's property, as is the land now occupied by **ROSE COTTAGES**, on the opposite (east) side of the Street.

Forbes Fisher had died in 1760, unmarried. The estate had passed to his sister Mary, the widow of Fairmedow Penyston. However, the plain old dwelling-house of Mary's ancestors had been deemed unsatisfactory: she had at once set about transforming it. By 1763, the house had been substantially extended and modernised. This was the mansion to which William Prowting had moved, presumably after the death of Mary Penyston. He was merely a leaseholder, the owner being Mary's son, Francis Penyston, who may never have lived here himself.

Jane Austen saw a good deal of the Prowtings. She refers in 1811 to a 'Gravel pit' which Mr Prowting had excavated 'just at the mouth of the approach to his House'. She felt that this might be a hazard to any visitor, although useful, perhaps, to her mother. It has been suggested that the site of the pit is marked to this day by the uneven surface on part of the lawn, at the end of the drive nearest the Street. However, the Tithe Map of 1840 shows such a pit (which may, by this time, have been turned into a pond) to have been close to the house itself, literally 'at the mouth of the approach'. Jane would not usually pass this way herself, though, for she is said to have taken a regular short cut to Prowtings across the adjoining meadow, climbing into it by means of a stile at the back of her own garden.

William Prowting died in 1821, aged 67. He had no surviving male issue, so his second daughter, Catherine Ann, inherited much of his estate. Catherine continued to live at Prowtings until her death in 1848, at the age of 65. According to tradition, Edward Knight had come to look upon this rather grand building as a rival manor-house. Much manorial property had been sold off in the 18th century by the absentee squires. Edward was eager to recover it. In 1822, he was able to acquire, from Mr Penyston, the reversion of the coveted Fisher property. In about 1850, within a couple of years of Catherine's death, Edward marked his disapproval by having the mansion pulled down, 'leaving only the offices, which were converted into a small farmhouse', and the old garden walls. By the end of the century, a modest dairy business was being run from here.

The part of the building that survived was its north-east corner. A plaque on the front commemorates its construction by 'M.P. 1763'. Interestingly, Mary Penyston had incorporated, on the north side, a wing of the original Morey house. Built of soft-red brick around a timber frame, this clearly dates from the 17th century or earlier. The then Fisher residence had been credited with six hearths in 1665: it had therefore been a house of comfortable size, although modest compared to Chawton House, which had twenty-one.

By the middle of the 20th century, Prowting's Farm had been parcelled off with other parts of the former Fisher holding and sold again. The 2,000-acre Chawton estate of Sir Richard Sharples, the Governor of Bermuda who was assassinated in 1973, included both Prowtings and Southfield Farm. It is said to have been his intention to retire to the compact little farmhouse. Instead, it was bought from his estate by Nicholas Kerridge in 1976. Mr Kerridge has restored the house to some of its former magnificence. A new wing has been built over the earlier foundations, incorporating the original vaulted cellar, which was discovered by the builders during their excavations. There has also been the addition of a Georgian-style porch. The renovation of the house was completed in 1985. Prowtings is now at least twice its former size, although the house of 1763, so familiar to Jane Austen (there was even a view of it from her attic stairs), appears to have been larger still. This is evident not only from the foundations (now buried), but also from the garden wall, which has been very visibly extended in order to connect with the newer wing.

The true seat of the Prowting family – part of the Stonehills tenement that they had acquired in 1670 – was the property known today as **ALPHONSUS HOUSE**. At the northern end of the village, a road called **Wolfe's Lane** (described in old documents as 'the road to Hartley') branches eastwards from the Street. Alphonsus House occupies the north-east corner of the junction. Its historic name is *Denmead*. This is preserved in the **DENMEAD COTTAGES**, on the opposite (south) corner of the junction, which likewise formed a part of the scattered Prowting estate. Denmead, alias Alphonsus House, was set in two acres of ground. These were crudely truncated by the by-pass in 1971. The present house, which is bounded on the west side by the Street and on the south by Wolfe's Lane, has evolved around a pair of old cottages which date from the 17th century or earlier. The original building is concealed under the south front, having been extended, on a grand scale, sometime between 1790 and 1810. The work was probably commissioned by William Prowting III after he had inherited the property in 1794 (he himself was already installed in the old Fisher house, soon to be known as 'Prowtings'), perhaps to provide a dignified marital home for one of his daughters. By the early part of the 20th century, Denmead had begun to be described, albeit unofficially, as 'the Dower House': John White refers to it as such in 1921.

It was at *Denmead* that Ann Mary Prowting, William's youngest daughter, had duly established herself in 1811, upon her marriage (aged about 23) to Captain Benjamin Clement, R.N., from Alton. Jane Austen was much in their company, but does not seem to have warmed to them. She writes in 1813, after accepting a lift in their carriage, that there had been 'civility on both sides; *I* would rather have walked, & no doubt, *they* must have wished I had'. On another occasion she writes cynically that 'The Clements are at home and are reduced to read'. Jane was content, nevertheless, to accept dairy products from Mrs Clement's cow. The Captain is described in 1817 as 'a very respectable, well-meaning man, without much manner', whilst his wife and sister are dismissed as 'all good humour and obligingness, and I hope (since the fashion allows it) with rather longer petticoats than last year'.

We have it on the authority of her niece that Jane took a keen interest in the affairs of her neighbours, and 'liked immensely to hear all about them. They sometimes served for her amusement, but it was her own nonsense that gave zest to the gossip ... The laugh she occasionally raised was by imagining for her neighbours impossible contingencies - by relating in prose or verse some trifling incident coloured to her own fancy ...' Her nephew and biographer refers moreover to her 'partiality for the Navy' and to 'the readiness and accuracy with which she wrote about it'. She had two brothers of her own in the service, and her naval figures are drawn with sympathy and affection. Why was she so disdainful of poor Clement? Not yet thirty when she first knew him, he comes across in her letters as being rather stiff and humourless, yet he was a brave and distinguished officer, in retirement from 1811 after an extraordinarily varied and eventful career. Late in life, he was to submit an enthusiastic account of it to the compiler of the *Royal Naval Biography*. At the age of 19 (though already a veteran of Camperdown and Copenhagen), he had been present at the Battle of Trafalgar, as a

Lieutenant in H.M.S. *Tonnant*. (He had spent much of that encounter clinging to the hull of an upturned jolly-boat - an alarming enough predicament for a non-swimmer, without the additional hazard of having a battle raging around one.) It is recounted that, a year later, whilst in command of a press gang in Jamaica, he had been seized by the collar and threatened with violence. 'Having a horse-whip in his hand, and feeling it necessary to act in self-defence, he immediately began to exercise the same upon the ruffian who had assaulted him, and very properly gave him a sound trimming.' Among other adventures, he had confronted mutinous crews, run aground, been cast adrift in an open boat, fought in a variety of other battles and skirmishes (in which he had been several times wounded), fallen through the burning roof of a house whilst tackling a raging fire, and suffered repeated bouts of disease. His own voice rings clearly through the account. Was Jane Austen regaled with his stories and put off by his lack of irony? Or was he, perhaps, a man of few words? Incidentally, as a great nephew of Gilbert White, Clement had a formidable literary connection of his own, though White's *Natural History of Selborne* was at that time little known about or read.

Captain Clement succeeded to the copyhold of Denmead after the death of his mother-in-law in 1832, and was immediately permitted by the Knights to purchase the freehold. He died in 1835. Mrs Clement lived out her days here, dying in 1858. The next owner of Denmead was their elder son, the Rev. Benjamin Clement. He died in 1873, and was succeeded in turn by his only sister, Ann Mary. 'Wolfe's Lane', originally a track through her property, is named after Ann Mary's husband, the painter George Wolfe, who died in 1883. The Wolfes are probably to be credited with the Victorian extension that faces the garden, including a bay window on two floors. Mrs Wolfe died in 1893, leaving Denmead to her unmarried niece and companion, Miss Lilias Edith Clement. This lady was the last of Prowting line at Chawton. After her death in 1895, at the age of 35, the estate was divided up and sold.

The Knight family, who in this way had re-acquired the freehold of Denmead, were then to use it as their Dower House (it was the residence, after 1914, of the widowed Mrs Montagu Knight), but they had sold it again by 1951. The building had acquired a third name by 1960, when it was called *Carlyle House*. It was taken over in that year by the Redemptorist Fathers, the congregation of Roman Catholic priests, founded by Alfonso Liguori in 1732, whose mission is among the poor. Carlyle House is now called Alphonsus House in Liguori's honour. The **industrial buildings** across the road were erected by the Fathers in the 1960s, and extended in 1993. From here, they are publishers of Roman Catholic and ecumenical literature. The magnificent gardens of Alphonsus House are a modern creation, and include an 'archaeological excavation', not of any antiquity, as an ornamental feature.

As one heads south again in the direction of the village centre, the spacious villa on one's left was another Prowting possession. Confusingly, this is also called the **DOWER HOUSE**, although it has only been so named since the second half of the 20th century. This may be the house to which Jane Austen refers in a letter of December 1816. She reports that Mr Papillon 'has secured the refusal of the House which Mrs Baverstock at present occupies in Chawton & is to vacate soon, which is of course intended for Mrs Elizth Papillon'. This, she jokes, is a sure sign of his intention to propose to her. Although the property was more modestly sized in those days, the Papillons may well have obtained a lease of it. This is suggested by the fact that the Garniers, who lived there later in the century, were close relatives, by marriage, of the Papillon family.

Much like Alphonsus House, the present building is a fascinating *mélange* of architectural styles, for it incorporates a pair of detached cottages. One of these opened onto the Street - it is half-timbered and, according to a recent theory, may even be a 14th-century hall-house - whilst the other, which is perhaps of later date, was set back from it at a right angle. These once humble dwellings, which Jane Austen would have known, belonged to Catherine Prowting in 1840 and were occupied by E.F. Paxton, Esq. The Tithe Map suggests that the two cottages were not yet combined. The one adjacent to the Street seems already to have been enlarged, though, and presumably it had been dignified by the addition of its impressive, Georgian-style front. The garden was much smaller then. It was adjoined on the east and south sides by a large field called 'Hop Andrews', land which was, or had previously been, given over to the cultivation of hops. Catherine had leased Hop Andrews to Ann Clement, leaving Paxton with only the original cottage garden (the perimeters of which are still discernable) and adjoining stable-yard, which are at the back of the house.

Soon afterwards, the house seems to have been put to use as a ladies' seminary. By the end of the 19th century, however, having been acquired by the Knight family at the dismemberment of the Prowting estate, it had become the country residence of Colonel Sir Edward Bradford (1836–1911). A younger son of the Rector of West Meon, Sir Edward Bradford had served in the Indian Army since before the Mutiny, and had lost an arm to a tiger.

His first wife was a daughter of the younger Edward Knight. Bradford was created a baronet in 1902, shortly before his retirement as Chief Commissioner of the Metropolitan Police, an office which he had held since 1890. He is commemorated by a rousing memorial in Chawton Church. The Dower House was known in Sir Edward's day as 'Chawton Cottage', a name which has often been applied, unhistorically, to the Austen house. He had left his mark here by the addition of the mock-Tudor front, on the side of the building which overlooks the garden. The most recent alterations date from the early 1930s, when Colonel Knight added an upper floor to the passage which connected the two cottages. (The improvements were for the benefit of a new tenant, Miss Verner, whose sister, Mrs Ian Henderson, lived for many years at Carlyle House.) According to the plans from that time, the parlour of the old cottage beside the Street, with its large inglenook fireplace and bread oven, was used as the servants' hall. The most recent addition to the house has been the terrace. This is a creation of the present owners, Colonel and Mrs David Whitaker.

A garden, hopkiln, and the rather handsome pair of labourer's cottages now called **SPRINGFIELD**, on the opposite side of the Street, belonged in 1840 to the Baigent family. By contrast, its northerly neighbour, **BEAN TREE COTTAGE**, also dates from the 1930s. This was built by Miss Verner of Chawton Cottage, alias the Dower House, as accommodation for her gardener.

The '**GREY FRIAR' INN**, across the road from Jane Austen's house, dates only from the 19th century. The cottages which it replaced seem to have been held previously by a Mr Philmore, so it is possible that poor Miss Benn had lived here rather than in one of the Thatch Cottages. In its early days as a beerhouse and grocery (it was in business by 1870), the building was known as the 'Chawton Arms'. There had also, at one time, been the 'Good Intent' (at the northern end of the village, by **Ye Old Post Office**), but the keeping of alehouses had traditionally been discouraged at Chawton. In the past, it was normal for a would-be publican to trade from his or her own front room. The Manor Court Roll records that, in 1558, 'The Widows Crowcher and Bean and Naylor are fined three pence each for keeping ale houses'. In 1617, the Manor Court had agreed that they should be banned altogether, on pain of a very substantial fine. Perhaps the tenants had been fired by puritanical fervour to discourage the vices associated with drinking. It is more likely that they objected to the drunken and rowdy behaviour of travellers, and that their intention was to deny them any excuse to linger in the village. The parish's disapproval of public houses was to be reaffirmed in 1748. Prevailing attitudes would not prevent the conversion of Jane Austen's future home into the 'New Inn', which took place some time after 1769. The 'Grey Friar', like the 'New Inn', was to enjoy the approval of the squire, whose property it was.

The 'Grey Friar', holding a *cinquefoil* in one hand and a black bracelet, or rosary, in the other, is the crest that has been handed down through the various branches of the Knights of Chawton. This crest, and the associated arms, appear to have belonged originally to some entirely unrelated Knights and to have been 'usurped' by John Knight, the builder of Chawton House, to mark his assimilation into the gentry. In 1738, and again in 1812, the family's unauthorised use of these arms was nevertheless to receive the rather dubious endorsement of the College of Arms.

As for **THE AUSTEN HOUSE**, it was originally part of the row of substantial farmhouses that were occupied by the leading yeomanry of the manor. The house was built, around 1700, by John Alderslade the younger, Yeoman. In the 18th century it was known, in his memory, as 'Petty Johns'. It stands on, or very near, the site of an earlier Alderslade house, some of the foundations of which are thought to survive under the present garden. In 1759, the property was acquired from John's descendants by John Marchant, and ten years later it was bought by the squire, Thomas Knight, who turned it into a pub. The 'New Inn' was to close in 1787. Mr Knight was then to instal his bailiff, Bridger Seward, a well-to-do gentleman farmer in his own right (he was also the tenant of Pound Farm), who died in 1808. Seward's widow Mary moved out in 1809 (possibly to Chawton Cottage, alias the Dower House), upon the marriage of their daughter to the litigious James Hinton Baverstock. This enabled the Austen ladies and their friend, Martha Lloyd, to move in. Edward Austen was first to carry out some costly improvements, including the re-arrangement of windows and the construction of three additional bedrooms over the kitchen quarters at the back.

The Austens seem to have designated their new home 'the Chawton cottage', although it continued to be described in legal documents as the 'Late Inn'. It was to be occupied by Jane Austen's sister, Cassandra, until her death in 1845. It was then partitioned into dwellings for workmen. There appears to have been accommodation for three separate families, including, by 1861, that of William Stephens, the Welsh coachman at Chawton House. Between 1873 and 1909, part of the building served as premises for the Chawton Workingman's Improvement Club. William Stephens became its manager, whilst his wife, Mary, was its regular supplier of 'cleaning materials, coals &c.' (By 1885, the enterprising Stephens had moved on to manage the dairy at Prowting's Farm.) The building was acquired from the estate by Mr T. Edward Carpenter in 1948, and was opened as a museum, under the care of the Jane Austen Memorial Trust, in July 1949. An old photograph shows that a high, brick wall enclosed the garden. This must have replaced the 'high wooden fence' described by Caroline Austen, which 'shut out the road ... all the length of the little domain'. A relic of the building's early manifestation as the 'New Inn' is the blocked-up hatchway on the street-side, through which the barrels were unloaded into the cellar.

Throughout its history, the population of Chawton has been remarkably stable: 33 households in 1086, 34 in 1302, 32 in 1665. By 1841, the figure had swelled to 91, although this included those living around the Butts, on the outskirts of Alton. The number of households in Chawton today is around 156, an increase for which the modern developments are accountable.

Interestingly, none of the grand – or aggrandised – houses in the village is any older than the 18th century. It had been observed by the Rector in 1725 that there were 'no noblemen, gentlemen or persons of note' in the village, excepting, of course, himself. Presumably, almost everyone who lived here then would have laboured in some form on the land. Chawton was thereafter to experience a degree of 'gentrification', which is strongly reflected in its architecture.

Since the beginning of the 20th century, Chawton society has changed beyond recognition. It was noted in 1911 that, of all the families recorded here in 1729, only the Frenches (labourers) and the Knights (squires) remained. The Knights alone maintain a foothold here today. Few of Chawton's present-day residents are employed on the land, or even in the village; but the cramped cottages once associated with the labouring classes are now considered to be highly desirable residences. All who live here today are able to take considerable pride in the appearance of their village, in its rich historical associations, and in the worldwide significance of its contribution to English letters.

SELECT BIBLIOGRAPHY

Jane Austen's Letters, collected and edited by Deirdre Le Faye (Oxford, 1996).

Jane Austen Bi-Centenary, 1775–1817, Chawton, Hants. (1975).

My Aunt Jane Austen: A Memoir by Caroline Austen, with the Recollections of John White (The Jane Austen Society, 1991).

William and Richard Austen Leigh, *Jane Austen: A Family Record*, revised and enlarged by Deirdre Le Faye (London, 1989).

William Austen Leigh and Montagu Knight, *Chawton Manor and its Owners: A Family History* (London, 1911).

Mavis Batey, 'Places of Inspiration', *Country Life*, 1 September 1994.

'Chawton House, Hampshire', *Country Life*, 27 June 1903.

John Coates, *St Nicholas Church, Chawton, Hampshire: A Chronicle Covering Seven Centuries* (no date).

C. Cochrane, *The Lost Roads of Wessex* (Newton Abbot, 1969).

Christopher Currie, *An Archaeological and Historical Survey of the Landscape of Chawton Estate ... to A.D. 1700* (1995).

William Curtis, *Short History and Description of the Town of Alton* (1896).

Violet Hunt, *History of the Parish of Chawton from 1894* (Chawton, 1994).

Christopher Hussey, 'Chawton House, Hampshire', *Country Life*, 2 and 9 February 1945 .

'Knight of Chawton', in *Burke's Landed Gentry*, 18th Edition, Vol.II (London, 1969), pp.380–82.

John Marshall, *Royal Naval Biography* (London, 1835)

Edward Roberts *et al., Hampshire Houses, 1250 - 1700: Their Dating and Development* (Hampshire County Council, 2003).

E. Roberts and P. Grover, 'Elizabethan Riding Stables at Chawton and Their Context', *Proceedings of the Hampshire Field Club,* 52 (1997), pp.151-64.

Joan Smith, Chawton (1972).

Robin Vick, 'Jane Austen's House at Chawton', *The Jane Austen Society Report for 1995*, pp.18–21.

The Victoria County History of Hampshire, ed. W. Page, Vol.II (London, 1903), pp.496–501.

Rupert Willoughby, *Life in Medieval England*, 1066–1485 (Pitkin Pictorial Guides, 1997).

Rupert Willoughby, 'Sir Adam de Gurdon and the Pass of Alton', in Barbara Large ed., *The Best of '98: The Eighteenth Annual Writers' Conference* (1998).